Learn to Draw
Extreme Sports

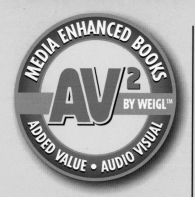

AV² provides enriched content that supplements and complements this book. Weigl's AV² books strive to create inspired learning and engage young minds in a total learning experience.

Your AV² Media Enhanced books come alive with...

Audio
Listen to sections of the book read aloud.

Key Words
Study vocabulary, and complete a matching word activity.

Video
Watch informative video clips.

Quizzes
Test your knowledge.

Embedded Weblinks
Gain additional information for research.

Slide Show
View images and captions, and prepare a presentation.

Try This!
Complete activities and hands-on experiments.

... and much, much more!

Go to **www.av2books.com**, and enter this book's unique code.

BOOK CODE

B 7 1 5 4 9 3

AV² by Weigl brings you media enhanced books that support active learning.

Published by AV² by Weigl
350 5th Avenue, 59th Floor
New York, NY 10118
Website: www.weigl.com   www.av2books.com

Library of Congress Cataloging-in-Publication Data

Extreme sports / edited by Heather Kissock.
     pages cm -- (Learn to draw)
ISBN 978-1-61913-239-9 (hardcover : alk. paper) -- ISBN 978-1-61913-244-3
(softcover : alk. paper)
1. Sports in art--Juvenile literature. 2. Athletes in art--Juvenile
literature. 3. Extreme sports--Juvenile literature. 4.
Drawing--Technique--Juvenile literature. I. Kissock, Heather.
NC825.S62E98 2012
743'.89796--dc23
                         2012000464

Printed in the United States of America in North Mankato, Minnesota
1 2 3 4 5 6 7 8 9 0 16 15 14 13 12

042012
WEP050412

Senior Editor: Heather Kissock
Art Director: Terry Paulhus

Every reasonable effort has been made to trace ownership and to obtain permission to reprint copyright material. The publishers would be pleased to have any errors or omissions brought to their attention so that they may be corrected in subsequent printings.

Weigl acknowledges Getty Images as its primary image supplier for this title.

3201300029338

Contents

2 . . . . AV² Book Code

4 . . . . Why Draw?

5 . . . . Extreme Sports

6 . . . . What is Formula One Car Racing?

10 . . . . What is Formula One Powerboating?

14 . . . . What is Moto X?

18 . . . . What is Rallying?

22 . . . . What is Skateboarding?

26 . . . . What is Snowmobiling?

30 . . . . Test Your Knowledge of Extreme Sports

31 . . . . Draw an Environment/ Glossary

32 . . . . Log on to av2books.com

6

10

14

18

22

26

Why Draw?

Drawing is easier than you think. Look around you. The world is made of shapes and lines. By combining simple shapes and lines, anything can be drawn. An orange is just a circle with a few details added. A flower can be a circle with ovals drawn around it. An ice cream cone can be a triangle topped with a circle. Most anything, no matter how complicated, can be broken down into simple shapes.

circle

oval

circle

circle

triangle

Drawing helps people make sense of the world. It is a way to reduce an object to its simplest form, say our most personal feelings and thoughts, or show others objects from our **imagination**. Drawing an object can help you learn how it fits together and works.

What shapes do you see in this car?

It is fun to put the world onto a page, but it is also a good way to learn. Learning to draw even simple objects introduces the skills needed to fully express oneself visually. Drawing is an excellent form of **communication** and improves people's imagination.

Practice drawing your favorite extreme sports equipment in this book to learn the basic skills necessary to draw. You can use those skills to create your own drawings.

Extreme Sports

The thrill of extreme sports attracts many fans. In extreme sports, people take part in high-risk activities. Most of these sports are performed at high speeds. They are often dangerous for the participants. For this reason, extreme athletes wear special gear and clothing to protect themselves.

Drawing the gear and clothing used in extreme sports is a useful way to learn how extreme athletes stay safe. It is also a way to learn how the equipment helps the athlete win races and perform stunts. As you draw the extreme sports in this book, think about what features the clothing and gear have that help protect athletes from injury.

What is Formula One Car Racing?

Formula One (F1) races are some of the fastest in the world. F1 racing cars are specially designed for speed. They can reach speeds as high as 215 miles (345 kilometers) per hour.

The races are held on either racetracks or public roads that have been closed for the event. A race is usually about 186 miles (300 km) long. The cars run laps around the course until they complete the mileage. The first car to cross the finish line is the winner.

Steering Wheel

The steering wheel of an F1 car is the driver's control center. It tells the driver the fuel levels and traveling speed. The wheel also holds a series of buttons that allow the driver to switch **gears** and change the position of the front wings.

Wings

An F1 car has wings on both its front and back ends. These wings make the car more **aerodynamic**. They help keep the car's tires on the road. They also help the car go around corners more quickly.

Suspension System

An F1 car's **suspension system** links the wings and the tires to the body of the car. It helps control the forces pushing on the car so that it stays steady on the course.

Seating
F1 cars are single-seaters. This means that only one person can fit inside the car. Its only seat is located in front of the engine.

Tires
There are two main types of tires for F1 cars. Each type has been built for certain driving conditions. Cars racing during wet weather will be fitted with tires that have a **tread**. The tread helps the car grip the road better. If cars are racing on a dry track, they are fitted with tires that have no tread. This allows them to go faster.

Engine
The engine of an F1 car is found close to the middle of the car. It runs on fuel that is very similar to the gas used in everyday cars.

How to Draw a Formula One Race Car

1 Start with a stick figure frame of the car. Use lines for the body and circles for the tires.

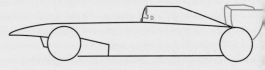

2 Now, draw the rear wing and engine, as shown.

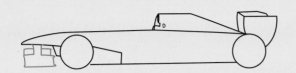

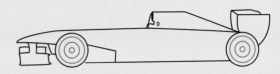

3 Next, draw the front wing.

4 Add details to the tires.

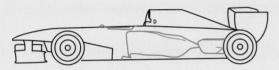

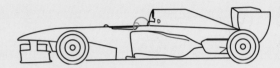

5 In this step, draw the stickers on the car.

6 Next, draw the Formula One driver.

7 Add details to the car, as shown.

8 Erase the extra lines and the stick figure.

9 Color the image.

What is Formula One Powerboating?

Formula One powerboating is closely related to F1 car racing. Specially designed boats race each other around a course set on water. This water can be in a lake, a river, or a bay. A racecourse is usually about 2,187 yards (2,000 meters) long.

An F1 powerboat can reach a speed of 100 miles (160 km) per hour in only four seconds. Powerboat drivers maneuver around tight turns and **straightaways**. All of their racing is done without changing gears or braking.

Size
F1 powerboats are 20 feet (6 m) long and 7 feet (2 m) wide. They weigh about 860 pounds (390 kilograms).

Hull
The boat has a tunnel hull design. This means that the boat has two hulls on either side of an open center. Air flows into the tunnel and keeps the boat **buoyant**. This helps the boat skim over the water.

Head and Neck Support

All F1 powerboat drivers are required to wear a head and neck support. Powerboats travel at such high speeds that a driver's head is pushed around with a great deal of force. Head and neck supports steady the driver's head during the race and help avoid injury.

Cockpit

Powerboat drivers sit in an enclosed cockpit. The cockpit is fitted with an airbag. It opens if the boat tips over during the race. This keeps the cockpit and the driver above water until rescue teams arrive.

Crash Boxes

Crash boxes sit along the sides of the powerboat. They are made of fiberglass and are meant to protect the boat and driver if there is a collision.

How to Draw a Formula One
Powerboat

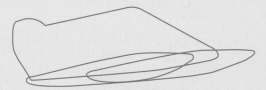

1 Start with a stick figure frame of the powerboat, as shown.

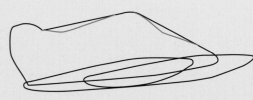

2 Now, draw the cockpit.

3 Then, draw the detail on the back of the boat.

4 Next, draw the screen of the cockpit.

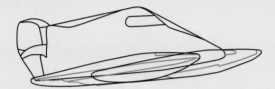

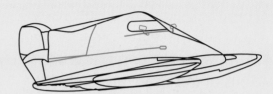

5 In this step, draw the hull on both sides of the powerboat.

6 Draw the mirrors and other details on the boat.

7 Add the stickers and the water.

8 Erase the extra lines and the stick figure.

9 Color the image.

What is Moto X?

Moto X, or motocross, is a sport that requires skill, determination, and balance. In this sport, athletes ride on specially designed motorcycles. They race these motorcycles over obstacles and along tracks. In some forms of the sport, athletes ride "freestyle." This means they perform tricks, such as flips and jumps, on obstacles and over walls.

Moto X riding is often done on public land. In these places, there are dirt trails and jumps where riders can practice tricks. Natural elements, such as mud holes, rocky ledges, and steep hills, are used as obstacles.

Seat
The long, flat seat on the bike is designed to allow riders to shift their weight quickly and provide more **traction** in corners.

Size
Most moto X bikes are smaller than traditional motorcycles. A moto X bike can be a **two-stroke** or four-stroke machine. Two-stroke bikes are lighter, more powerful, and noisier than four-stroke bikes. They are also less friendly to the environment.

Helmet

The helmet is the most important piece of safety equipment. When falling off a motorcycle, a rider's head can hit the ground. Helmets have saved riders from serious head injury.

Goggles

Many riders wear goggles to protect their eyes from the dirt that flies up from the track. To land safely, riders need to see clearly as they make jumps and do stunts. Goggles ensure they can do this.

Gloves

Gloves help the riders grip the bike's handles, seats, and other parts of the motorcycle. They also protect the rider's hands if the rider falls in the hard dirt.

Suspension

Moto X bikes have plenty of suspension. This allows riders to tackle large jumps and ride at a higher speed over the rough course.

How to Draw an Moto X Bike

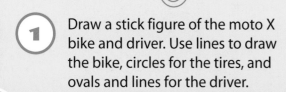

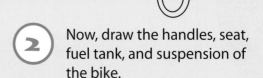

1 Draw a stick figure of the moto X bike and driver. Use lines to draw the bike, circles for the tires, and ovals and lines for the driver.

2 Now, draw the handles, seat, fuel tank, and suspension of the bike.

(3) Next, draw the moto X driver.

(4) Draw the driver's helmet.

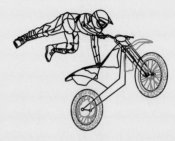

(5) In this step, add details to the driver's gear.

(6) Draw the mudguard in the front of the bike, and add details to the tires.

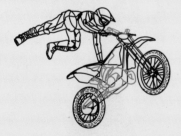

(7) Complete the handle, and draw the engine and other parts of the bike, as shown.

(8) Erase the extra lines and the stick figure.

(9) Color the image.

What is Rallying?

Rallying, or rally car racing, features street cars racing on specially designed courses. These courses include both streets and off-road areas. This type of racing is often challenging for drivers and entertaining for spectators.

Rally races take place in summer and winter. They cover hundreds of miles (kilometers) and last many hours. This extreme test of skill, speed, and **endurance** gives rally car drivers the reputation of being among the best drivers in the world.

Steel Tubes

Rally cars have very strong steel tubes called roll bars inside. The tubes are designed to keep the driver safe if the car crashes or rolls over.

Tires

Tires are one of the most important parts of a rally car. There are special tires for driving at very high speeds on asphalt, loose gravel, sand, dirt, snow, and ice. Tires will last longer if they have the proper tread for the types of surfaces the car will be traveling on.

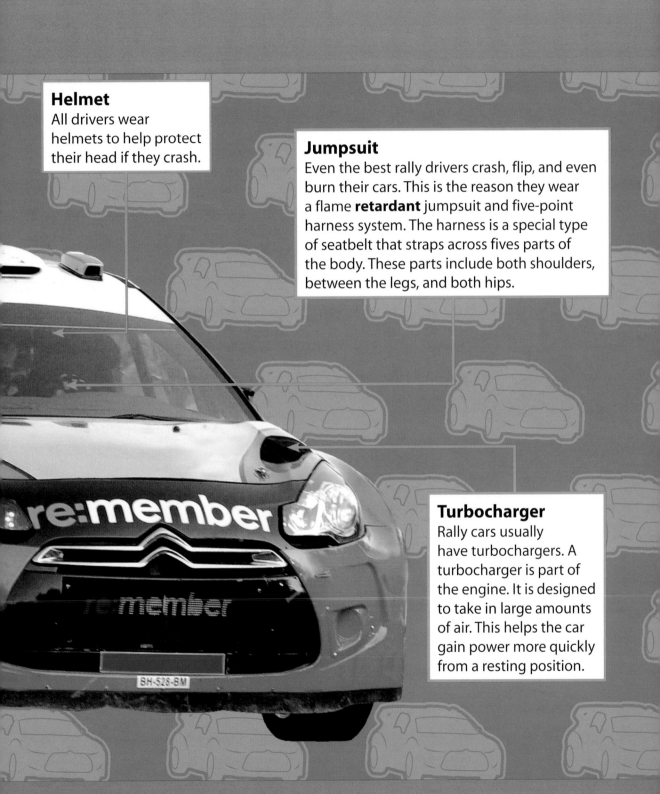

Helmet
All drivers wear helmets to help protect their head if they crash.

Jumpsuit
Even the best rally drivers crash, flip, and even burn their cars. This is the reason they wear a flame **retardant** jumpsuit and five-point harness system. The harness is a special type of seatbelt that straps across fives parts of the body. These parts include both shoulders, between the legs, and both hips.

Turbocharger
Rally cars usually have turbochargers. A turbocharger is part of the engine. It is designed to take in large amounts of air. This helps the car gain power more quickly from a resting position.

How to Draw a
Rally Car

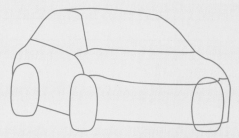

1 Draw a stick figure frame of the rally car. Use lines for the body and ovals for the tires.

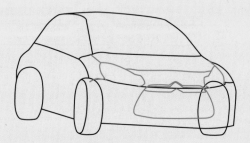

2 Now, draw the lights and front bumper.

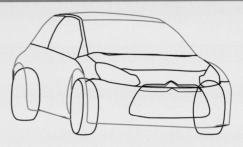

3 Next, draw the windshield and window screens.

4 Draw the roof of the car and the fenders.

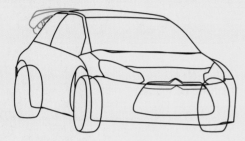

5 In this step, draw the wing at the back of the car.

6 Add details to the tires.

7 Draw the back mirror and stickers, and add details to the door, lights, bumper, and roof of the car.

8 Erase the extra lines and the stick figure.

9 Color the image.

What is Skateboarding?

Skateboarding was developed in the 1950s. At first, it was called sidewalk surfing. This is because the sport resembled surfing, but took place on land.

Skateboarders use their boards to do a variety of tricks, including **ollies** and other jumps. Some of their moves require high speeds. This increases the risk of injury.

Helmet

A helmet is the most important piece of equipment a skateboarder can wear. Falls are common in skateboarding. The helmet protects the skateboarder's head if it comes in contact with a hard surface, such as concrete.

Wheels

Most skateboard wheels are made from hard rubber. Their size depends on how the skateboard is to be used. Tricks such as flips and kicks are easier to do with small, lightweight wheels. Vert, or ramp, boarders use larger wheels. These wheels allow the board to reach higher speeds and maintain a good grip on the ramp.

Deck

The deck of a skateboard is the part that the boarder stands on. It normally has upturned ends and dips through the middle. This design gives the boarder more control over the board when performing tricks.

Pads
Knee pads and elbow pads protect the body when falls take place. There are fewer scrapes and bruises when pads are used.

Shoes
Most skateboarders wear skate shoes instead of sneakers. These specially designed shoes have a large, flat bottom. This allows the skateboarder's feet to better grip the board. These shoes are often **reinforced** in areas that normally wear down quickly when skateboarding.

Trucks
Trucks are attached to the bottom of the board. Trucks are **axles**. They allow the wheels to turn and move in the direction the boarder wants to go.

23

How to Draw a
Skateboarder

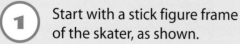

1 Start with a stick figure frame of the skater, as shown.

2 Now, draw the face and helmet of the skater.

3 Next, draw the skater's arms, legs, and body.

4 Draw the skateboard.

5 In this step, draw the hair and jacket of the skater.

6 Complete the skater's face by drawing the eyes, nose, and mouth.

7 Draw the skateboard wheels and the skater's elbow guards, knee pads, and sneakers.

8 Erase the extra lines and the stick figure.

9 Color the image.

What is Snowmobiling?

Snowmobiling is a sport that requires skill, strength, and courage. Snowmobilers race across the snow on a fast, heavy machine called a snowmobile. These machines can travel at speeds faster than 100 miles (160 km) per hour.

There are many types of snowmobiles. Some are designed for racing. Others are made for performing jumps and tricks.

Skis
A pair of skis at the front steer the snowmobile through the snow. The driver uses hand controls to guide the skis through the snow.

Helmet

Special helmets protect the head and face from injuries if a rider crashes or is thrown from the snowmobile. Other safety equipment includes goggles, chest pads, shoulder pads, and knee pads.

Clothing

Snowmobiling is a winter sport, so protection from cold weather is needed. A warm jacket, pants, gloves, socks, and boots keep the snowmobiler warm.

Track

A track or tread at the back of the snowmobile rotates to push the vehicle forward.

How to Draw a
Snowmobile

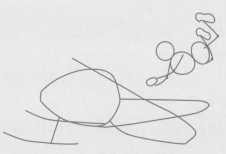

1 Draw the stick figure of the snowmobile and rider.

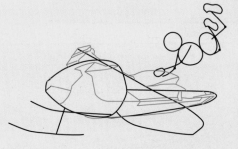

2 Now, draw the snowmobile, as shown

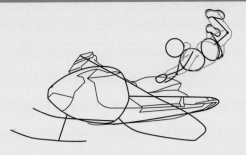
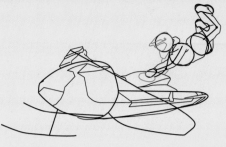

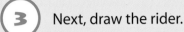

3 Next, draw the rider.

4 Draw the helmet of the rider and the seat of the snowmobile.

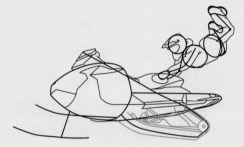
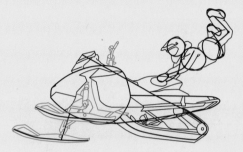

5 In this step, draw the tracks.

6 Draw the handle and skis of the snowmobile.

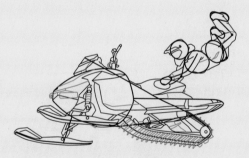

7 Now, add details to the tracks and other parts of the snowmobile, as shown.

8 Erase the extra lines and the stick figure.

9 Color the image.

Test Your Knowledge of Extreme Sports

1.
How fast can an F1 car travel?

Answer: About 215 miles (345 km) per hour

2.
What style of hull do F1 powerboats have?

Answer: A tunnel hull

3.
What part of a moto X bike allows riders to shift their weight quickly?

Answer: The long, flat seat

4.
What part of a rally car's engine helps it gain power?

Answer: The turbocharger

5.
When did skateboarding begin?

Answer: In the 1950s

6.
What does a snowmobile's back tread do?

Answer: It pushes the snowmobile forward.

Want to learn more? Log on to av2books.com to access more content.

Draw an Environment

Materials
- Large white poster board
- Internet connection or library
- Pencils and crayons or markers
- Glue or tape

Steps
1. Complete one of the extreme sports drawings in this book. Cut out the drawing.
2. Using this book, the internet, and a library, find out about your sport and the environment in which it is performed.
3. Think about what might be in this environment. What does the environment look like? What sorts of objects are found near it? What needs to be in the environment for the sport to be performed?
4. On the large white poster board, draw an environment in which your sport might take place. Be sure to place all the features you noted in step 3.
5. Place the cutout sport in its environment with glue or tape. Color the environment to complete the activity.

Glossary

aerodynamic: shaped to allow air to flow smoothly over it

axles: the pins or bars on which wheels rotate

buoyant: able to float

communication: the sending and receiving of information

endurance: the ability or strength to last

gears: the parts of a car that allow it to reach certain speeds

imagination: the ability to form new creative ideas or images

ollies: maneuvers in skateboarding in which the skater kicks the tail of the board down while jumping in order to make the board pop into the air

reinforced: to strengthen by adding material

retardant: a substance that reduces the rate of action

straightaways: parts of a course that extend in a straight line, without a turn or curve

suspension system: a system of springs that supports the body of a wheeled vehicle

traction: the friction between a wheel and a surface

tread: the grooved surface of a tire

two-stroke: relating to an internal combustion engine whose piston makes two strokes for every explosion

Log on to www.av2books.com

AV² by Weigl brings you media enhanced books that support active learning. Go to www.av2books.com, and enter the special code found on page 2 of this book. You will gain access to enriched and enhanced content that supplements and complements this book. Content includes video, audio, weblinks, quizzes, a slide show, and activities.

Audio
Listen to sections of the book read aloud.

Video
Watch informative video clips.

Embedded Weblinks
Gain additional information for research.

Try This!
Complete activities and hands-on experiments.

WHAT'S ONLINE?

 Try This!

Complete an interactive drawing tutorial for each of the six extreme sports in the book.

 Embedded Weblinks

Learn more about each of the six extreme sports in the book.

 Video

Watch a video about extreme sports.

EXTRA FEATURES

 Audio
Listen to sections of the book read aloud.

 Key Words
Study vocabulary, and complete a matching word activity.

 Slide Show
View images and captions, and prepare a presentation.

 Quizzes
Test your knowledge.

AV² was built to bridge the gap between print and digital. We encourage you to tell us what you like and what you want to see in the future.

Sign up to be an AV² Ambassador at www.av2books.com/ambassador.

Due to the dynamic nature of the Internet, some of the URLs and activities provided as part of AV² by Weigl may have changed or ceased to exist. AV² by Weigl accepts no responsibility for any such changes. All media enhanced books are regularly monitored to update addresses and sites in a timely manner. Contact AV² by Weigl at 1-866-649-3445 or av2books@weigl.com with any questions, comments, or feedback.